Adapted from "Treaty words—for as long as the rivers flow," by Aimée Craft, originally
published in *ndncountry* Fall 2018, Vol. 41 No. 2 by Prairie Fire Press and Contemporary Verse 2.

Cover art by Luke Swinson, designed by Paul Covello
Interior design by Paul Covello
Edited by Mary Beth Leatherdale

Annick Press Ltd.

We acknowledge the support of the Canada Council for the Arts and the Ontario Arts Council,
and the participation of the Government of Canada/la participation du gouvernement du
Canada for our publishing activities.

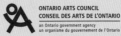

Library and Archives Canada Cataloguing in Publication

Title: Treaty words : for as long as the rivers flow / Aimée Craft ; illustrations by Luke Swinson.
Names: Craft, Aimée, 1980- author. | Swinson, Luke, 1989- illustrator.
Identifiers: Canadiana (print) 20200328387 | Canadiana (ebook) 20200328832 | ISBN 9781773214962
(hardcover) | ISBN 9781773214979 (HTML) | ISBN 9781773214986 (PDF) | ISBN 9781773214993 (Kindle)
Subjects: LCSH: Indigenous peoples—Legal status, laws, etc.—Canada—Juvenile literature. | LCSH:
Indigenous peoples—Canada—Government relations—Juvenile literature. | CSH: Native peoples—Canada—
Claims—Juvenile literature.
Classification: LCC E92 .C73 2021 | DDC j342.7108/72—dc23

Published in the U.S.A. by Annick Press (U.S.) Ltd.
Distributed in Canada by University of Toronto Press.
Distributed in the U.S.A. by Publishers Group West.

Printed in China

annickpress.com
aimeecraft.ca
lukeswinsonart.com

Also available as an e-book.
Please visit annickpress.com/ebooks for more details.

THIS BOOK IS DEDICATED TO
THOSE WHO WILL COME NEXT . . .
THE TEACHERS AND THE LEARNERS.
—A.C.

FOR MY WONDERFUL NIECE, INGRID.
—L.S.

She sat there, on the bank of the kitchi sipi with her Mishomis, watching the wide river pass them by.

This was their place.

He had lived there all his life, watching his children and his grandchildren grow. Mishomis's house was small but that didn't matter, because most of his time was spent out on the land, in the bush, and when he could, on the mighty river.

Even though she had grown up in the city, it was this small lot, with banks that collapsed into the river, that was the closest thing to home for her.

In his lifetime Mishomis had traveled that river many times, up and down, until the dams were built. Then the river changed. Even so, after the dams blocked his canoe, he continued to spend time on and with the river. It was his place. His relative.

Throughout his life he had helped research the nameo—the sturgeon—in the river and restock the population. In his later years he had led territorial mapping projects of original place names in Anishinaabemowin, recalling each place by its original name and significance.

Every spring, while there was still snow on the ground, he would cash in his pension check, buy supplies, and head into the bush. He'd take only a backpack, some flour, sugar, lard, and tea and would come back out four to six weeks later, hitchhiking his way home.

She would get a short call from him saying that he was back, and she'd make her way up to visit him.

On these and other visits, they sat, looking across and at the river, sometimes talking to each other, but more often sitting in silence, listening. The beauty of their silence was in everything that they heard around them.

Mishomis taught her how to hear, challenging her to understand each sound, from the most pronounced bird calls to the subtle sound of tiny insects crawling around in the grass.

One particular spring, which followed a winter with more snow and cold weather than in previous years, she went to visit him. He had come back from his spring trip, but much of the land still rested under thin, interspersed pockets of snow.

They sat on the tall bank of the river facing east, looking toward the other distant bank.

He recounted tales of snaring rabbits, finding old camps, building fires, drinking tea, hearing a baby moose being born, and eating fresh fish from the small spring-fed lakes.

Then they sat and let the silence speak.

They were surrounded by the tall grass swaying in the wind, the midday sun warming their faces.

The trees were making their spring sounds, popping and cracking, the snow blowing by and whooshing against her skin, and spring birds making their small and distinctive calls.

The geese honked as they flew over, telling her and Mishomis that they had seen them. The geese wanted them to know that they'd made it home.

They heard all of these sounds above that of the ice breaking, at once subtle and deafening, calming and distracting.

Every sound was outside and inside of them. They knew that all of this would be happening with or without them, that they were such a small part of Creation.

Although the sun was warm, Mishomis set out to build a small fire. That was usually a sign that someone would be by to visit or that they might be sitting out for another long while. The fire was to keep them warm and make tea, but mostly it was a place to hold their gaze as they told stories and jokes or as they sat in silence.

While he was building the fire, she walked closer to the bank and lay down on a sun-warmed rock. As the popping and crackling of the river subsided, it was replaced by twinkling sounds of ice crystals breaking up.

With her eyes closed she could see the golden light through her eyelids and knew that the sun—the original grandfather—and the ice were working together to rejoin the flowing river water.

When she came back to sit by the fire with Mishomis, she told him about the sounds, and how it had lifted her spirit to see the ice and the sun working together, making change. It was such a special event to witness.

She knew it was a privilege to be there in that moment, witnessing this intense transition. And she thought about all of the time that her Mishomis spent out on the land listening to these sounds.
Every year, since his birth.

He turned to her, lovingly reminding his granddaughter that she had responsibilities to this land and water, and to their stories.

With an exaggerated hand gesture, he made a full circle to acknowledge everything around him. He repeated the hand gesture and explained:

"This is why the Treaty is for as long as the sun shines, the grass grows, and the rivers flow."

She nodded in affirmation. She knew that it was their way of explaining the concept of foreverness during the making of Treaty.

He paused to put a few more logs on the fire.

"When the earth was created, it was a partnership between the earth realm and the sky realm. With the help of Creator, our grandfather sun and grandmother moon agreed to work together with our mother, the earth, to create life. Then other beings of Creation were placed on the earth and in the sky. We, humans, Anishinaabe, were the last to be placed here. This is why we refer to ourselves as younger brothers and sisters to the rest of the beings in Creation."

Lowering his voice a bit, Mishomis leaned toward her.

"You know, my girl, that my granny was a little girl when the Treaty was made. She remembered. She would talk to me about the sounds and smells of the camp. All the people assembled there. Cooking, visiting, laughing, talking, smoking the pipes, and the jiiskaan ceremonies. They were all there. They had asked to make the Treaty. And they knew how to make good treaties."

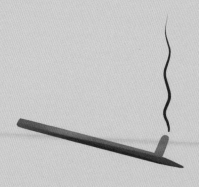

She looked back onto the river, at the sheets of ice now caving into the river, under the surface of the fast-moving water.

The twinkling, crystalline sounds were now more like a symphony with high notes of clashing cymbals and breaking ice, bass drums pounding with the ice sheets plunging into the water, and the soft string melodies of the water resurfacing, gently flowing and surging.

It also made her think of the sounds of ceremony: the eagle whistles, the drum, the shakers. It made her think, *We really are replicating the sounds of nature through our music and celebrations, all of which help heal us.*

Her Mishomis broke into her thoughts with his words.

"We made those treaties because we were taught to make treaties. Treaties are the basis of all relationships. We learned them from everything around us. That was the gift the Creator gave us. We spent many years listening and observing—to see how good treaty relationships were made. We use the word aagooiidiwin to explain the Treaty: it means that we agree to work together."

She stood to warm her hands by the fire. Mishomis carried on:

"Long ago, we made treaties with our brothers and sisters, the animal nations . . . You remember those stories don't you? We made those treaties to live well together. With the deer nation, for example, we agreed not to take too many of them. In turn they would provide us with food and sustenance. We agreed to work together. To collaborate and respect each other. We agreed that we would discuss when we did not agree and find solutions together. That treaty built upon all the other treaties that came before. We promised that we would always do our best to honor the treaty. To do that, we would meet regularly to confirm our agreement to continue to act in relationship, and toward mino-biimaadiiziwin, that collective and reciprocal sense of well-being. We would all benefit from the relationship, as equals. And most of all, we would respect each other, always. Without the respect, there could be no treaty."

Mishomis's voice was growing louder. She wanted to look at him, but was afraid she would interrupt his teaching, so she kept her eyes on the fire.

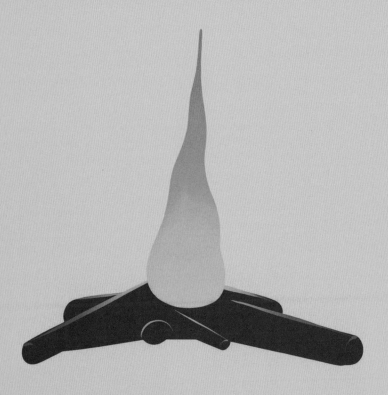

"In the Treaty we made with the Queen we had an agreement to work together. Everything we negotiated with the Crown is on top of what we already had. What the Queen's children misunderstood was that they thought that they owned the land and that they controlled us through the Treaty. They did not respect us. But we have always known that we retained our sovereignty, laws, language, connection to the land, and ways of being. We agreed through the Treaty that we would live well side by side."

Mishomis paused to throw some tea bags in the boiling water.

"As I said, the first treaty that was made was between the earth and the sky. It was an agreement to work together. We build all of our treaties on that original treaty. And that's what we said to the Crown when they came to discuss how we would live together on this land: for as long as the sun shines, the grass grows, and the rivers flow. Like the original treaty."

The young girl and her Mishomis sat in silence. She listened to the flow of the river and the wind moving around in the grass, and she felt her face warm with the glow of the fire and the spring sun.

This was the original treaty.

With her eyes closed she tried to link the pieces of the story together. She was ashamed that she couldn't sit there and listen to his stories in Anishinaabemowin.

He offered words in the language, which he inserted into English sentences for her benefit. She knew she had missed an important part of what it was to grow and truly understand her place in Creation, something each generation until her own had been able to know and feel.

She knew that each word carried a meaning and a teaching. She tried to think of each element of his stories in the language: geezis, akiin, nibi, sipi, wabesheshi, ishkode.

They all resonated in her mind and stirred
her heart as she sat on the bank of that river.

Her Mishomis spoke again, in a softer voice:

"The Creator also showed us how to remember. By having the sun rise every day, the earth and the sky are renewing their commitment to work together. And we in turn honor that relationship and directly benefit from it."

As she looked out at the water that was starting to overtake the ice, she could see that the treaty was coming to life.

There had been a period of rest over the winter, followed by a delicate dance of reciprocity and respect between the ice and the sun, resulting in a renewal of life for all living things in Creation.

This was natural law in action.
By observing it, she was part of it.

As the day progressed and the sun moved toward the west it dawned on her that Mishomis might not have many more seasons to live. He was sharing his teachings, parts of the bundle he carried, for her to bring forward and to share with those who would come next.

Although the responsibility for these stories could sometimes feel like a burden, she understood that they were also a great gift.

The fire was falling to embers. Mishomis didn't add any more wood to it. She knew they'd done their work for the day. There would be no visitors, other than the Creation that surrounded them, their silence, and their words.

Mishomis spoke again:

"Every person was born with a set of spiritual instructions or understandings, my girl. It's what we do with it that defines us as human beings. You see, as humans, we were given a name, a clan, a way of life, but most importantly the ability to exercise free will, to choose whether or not to pick up that way of life. We were given the ability to learn from our relatives on this earth about their treaty relationships and through what we call natural law, or earth's law."

It was as though he had read her mind. And then she laughed out loud.

He was not reading her mind. They were both hearing the land and everything that was surrounding them.

He joined in her laughter. She was grateful for such a day.

She knew that for the rest of her life she would come to this river to remember the original treaty relationship and the deeper meaning of respect, reciprocity, and renewal:

for as long as the sun shines, the grass grows, and the rivers flow.

AUTHOR'S NOTE

Since I was a young girl, I have been taught to listen and observe. There is so much to learn from everything that is around us. It helps us better understand what's inside of us as human beings.

When we truly listen, we can hear that Creation has a way of being: what we sometimes call natural law. All beings have a part to play in making sure Mother Earth continues to thrive. There are unspoken and unwritten agreements between all parts of Creation. Over time our Anishinaabe ancestors modeled themselves on this natural law and formed customs that make us who we are and that help us to understand our place in Creation.

The story in this book reflects how natural law gives us an understanding of treaties, or what I call "agreements to make relationships" that would allow us (Indigenous and settler) to live well together, in harmony, in accordance with those laws. In particular, this story reminds us that our treaties are anchored in relationships based on respect, responsibility, and renewal. Respect for each other, ongoing responsibilities toward one another, and a constant renewal and affirmation of that relationship. What our ancestors promised was an equal and nonexploitative sharing of the land, for the benefit of everyone, including all the other beings that belong to the land as well: the trees, the rocks, the water, the four-legged animals, the winged ones, the crawlers, the swimmers, everyone!

Today each of us must think about all of these relationships and how our actions will affect all of our relations.

Treaties are not just words written on paper or empty promises. They are not contracts for the sale of land. They are the agreements by which our ancestors confirmed that we would share these lands, without interference but with respect for each other. Today, we need to better understand these values and renew these relationships which build on all of the relationships that have existed for millennia between all parts of Creation. These relationships help us understand our responsibilities in these territories we call home.

Aimée Craft

Aimée Craft is an Anishinaabe/Métis lawyer from Treaty 1 territory in Manitoba. She is an Associate Professor at the Faculty of Common Law, University of Ottawa and a leading researcher on Indigenous laws, treaties, and water.

Luke Swinson is an Anishinaabe illustrator who is a member of the Mississaugas of Scugog Island First Nation. He lives in Kitchener, ON.